T0193590

FROM
SADNESS
TO
SALVATION

MAXINE BROWN

Copyright © 2022 Maxine Brown.

All rights reserved. No part of this book may be used or reproduced by any means, graphic, electronic, or mechanical, including photocopying, recording, taping or by any information storage retrieval system without the written permission of the author except in the case of brief quotations embodied in critical articles and reviews.

Balboa Press books may be ordered through booksellers or by contacting:

Balboa Press
A Division of Hay House
1663 Liberty Drive
Bloomington, IN 47403
www.balboapress.com
844-682-1282

Because of the dynamic nature of the Internet, any web addresses or links contained in this book may have changed since publication and may no longer be valid. The views expressed in this work are solely those of the author and do not necessarily reflect the views of the publisher, and the publisher hereby disclaims any responsibility for them.

Any people depicted in stock imagery provided by Getty Images are models, and such images are being used for illustrative purposes only.
Certain stock imagery © Getty Images.

ISBN: 979-8-7652-2775-6 (sc)
ISBN: 979-8-7652-2776-3 (e)

Print information available on the last page.

Balboa Press rev. date: 06/10/2022

Contents

A. Acknowledgements

I would like to take this time, to acknowledge the people –who have been inspirational in my life and have helped me along the way.

First, I would like to thank my Lord and Savior Jesus Christ for steering me in this direction to become a writer, and to be able to help me inspire others

Secondly, I thank my parents- Jean and Jessie Brown, Sr., who are my guardian angels- watching from above. I thank them for the great influencing that they have always instilled in me. I thank God daily for knowing them, and for all of the joyful times that we were able to share together.

Thirdly, a huge thanks to my daughter Chantel, who has helped me along the way. I thank God for her fine expertise in the IT systems arena, and that has really helped me a lot.

Lastly, I thank my friend and prayer partner Mrs. Mary Terry. Since the inception of when we first met, about ten years ago, I can say that Mrs. Mary exemplifies what it means to have a close friend.

B. FOREWORD

"Maxine Brown is a beautiful friend. I have come to admire her through the years, and have great respect for her strong sense of mission that she has devoted herself to fulfill, and several areas of her life. She truly has an unwavering seriousness of purpose to help people, by sharing the wisdom that she's learned through her life experiences.

This book's message will be invaluable to those dealing with loss and sorrow, offering much hope and comfort, as Maxine shares how she was able to find peace and salvation for each trial that she had to walk through, with the help of her Lord and Savior, Jesus Christ, prayer, and the compassion and kindness of others.

I am grateful to know this woman of God, and believe that her book will testify to what God can do in your life. As you read her story, expect your heart to be touched, inspired, and greatly encouraged."

Donna Lee Nefferdorf, Chaplin and Author, February 27, 2022

"Miss Maxine J. Brown is a loving mother, grandmother, dear friend, and a motivational spiritual leader. I had the pleasure of meeting this beautiful woman through her gorgeous daughter, Chantel Brown-Williams. She wrote an amazing book, "Walking in Divine Health-Gracefully," which empowered me to take control of my health and reconnect with a higher power. Miss Maxine loves visiting the rock garden near her home, and helping children with their studies, provide positive affirmations, encourage people to be kind, serve others, and lead by example.

She always takes time out of her day to spread love to those close to her as well as strangers. Her new book, "From Sadness to Salvation," will be a treat to others because it illustrates how God help her to inspire others."

Denise Allen-Pineda, February 27, 2022

C. Introduction

My name is Maxine Janet Brown, I am the founder of "From Sadness to Salvation." This book details how I overcame obstacles that were very detrimental in some cases where some people would have thrown in the towel and given up, but I thank God that I was able to overcome many of the situations and live my life to the fullest. And I truly hope that you will find help and revelation as you read my book.

D. DEDICATION

I would like to dedicate this book first to my Lord and Savior, Jesus Christ, he is the one who made all of this possible and allowed me to bring "From Sadness to Salvation" to fruition. I am thankful that I can share with you all some of life's challenges that I have faced.

Secondly, I would like to dedicate this book to my parents- the late Jean Lou and Jessie James Brown, Sr. Throughout my life, they have taught and instilled morals in me that are very much prevalent today. It is because of them that I am able to write my third book.

E. ABOUT ME

Hello, my name is **Maxine Janet Brown**. I was born in a rural area on the Eastern Shore of Virginia in 1962. Since then, I have witnessed many milestones all of which has brought forth much wisdom, strength, and knowledge. My parents were great, and always cherished family, spirituality, and hard work. I will forever miss the late Jean and Jessie Brown, Sr.!

I am the eldest of five siblings; Nancy, Shirley, Jessie, Jr., and Rebecca, whom all of them I love and adore. Each of them represents a different yet unique personality. I am the proud mother of a very amazing daughter, who I like to call a trailblazer-Chantel Williams, and a very dedicated and hardworking son-in-law Alexander Williams, Jr. From this union, I was blessed with my first grandchild-Alexander Williams, III (Tre'). They are very dear to me.

I received my elementary and secondary education in Accomack County public school. I then went on to further my education by receiving my Associate's degree in Early Childhood Education from Eastern Shore community college in 2004. Very early in life I accepted that my spiritual gift was teaching because I was given the responsibility to care for my siblings while my parents were at work. It also gave me the experience of working with other people and finding out what their interests were.

Following my degree completion at ESCC, I decided to pursue my education a little further and became a student at the University of Cincinnati's distance learning/online program. I received a Bachelor's Degree in Early Childhood Education. This was an amazing year because my daughter also received her Bachelor's Degree from Virginia State University in Computer Information Systems. We are each other's biggest accountability partner! Over the years, I have had the privilege in teaching in various capacities to include, but not limited to daycare, learning centers, public schools, home-based, churches, etc. I am currently a retired teacher of 36 years from the Wicomico County School District.

F. RELEASED FROM WORK

Around June 2000, I went to work as normal. Performing my duties as usually as a supervisor in the educational department. Then as my shift was about to be over, I was told that I would be terminated from my position. I was devastated, as if the wind was knocked out of me. I tried to maintain my composure. I started to question in my mind, "Did I do something wrong?" "Did I come to work late some days?" "What could it be?!"

When I asked, no real explanation was given to me. However, I was given job duties to perform that were not even close to my job description. I was to complete this job that was closely related to doing payroll. And it was to be completed by Friday that week. Well, I did the work, and worked as diligently as I could, because I had a young daughter to consider- who was in school at the time.

Pat-Pat did well in school, and she excelled in all of her school/ educational endeavors. And I wanted to ensure that I was still able to adhere to her continued school years, until she graduated. Thus, I took on employment at a local produce market as a book keeper. This job continued, for a few years- until Pat-Pat graduated and went on to college.

G. Car Accidents

During the summer of 2008, I was involved in my first vehicle accident. I was in Va. at the time, and I was on my way back to Salisbury, Md., because I had to teach school that day. When, my car was hit on sudden impact by another driver who did not give any signals or indications that she was changing lanes. My vehicle spun around in the road, and ended up in the median strip. I was really shaken up. At this time, my air bags deployed. And my car was a total loss!

Then during the summer of June 2011, I endured my second vehicle accident. At this time I was in Salisbury, Md. The motorist was using her cell phone, and probably did not pay attention to the fact that I was blowing my horn- as an indication that she was traveling too close to me. I ended up slamming into a reduced speed limit sign. And my windshield shattered, causing the paramedics to vacuum the pieces of shard glass off my clothes, before I could be transported to the hospital.

H. No Vehicle

Well, for about 6 months- I was without a vehicle. This was something that was new for me. My neighbor would often provide rides for me. She was very helpful and reliable. I would often ride to the store or where ever I needed to go with my neighbor. Or sometimes I would seek public transportation. Of course, this was something that I really wasn't used to, because I always had a car, and I would drive myself to places that I needed to go.

I thank God that I eventually got a new vehicle.

I. Ram in the Bush

On many occasions, I would walk outside to the area where my new car would be. I would put some anointing oil there and say, "Lord, I thank You for the Cadillac that You are going to bless me with!" Well, this continued for the remainder of the six months that I was without a vehicle.

J. A Great Car Dealer

I had acquired enough money for a down payment on a car. So I went to a nearby automobile store. Upon walking into the car store, I was greeted by a great car dealer- Mr. Elton. After, looking at many vehicles on the lot, Mr. Elton said, "Ms. Maxine here is one that you might like!" I test drove the car. And I really liked it.

Upon further observation of the features that the car had to offer, I noticed the brand of the vehicle was a Dodge Ram. Even though, I prayed and thanked God for the car, He had another "Ram in the Bush!" I kept that car for five years-until I purchased the car that I have now. I love this car, and I've been told that it looks much similar to a Cadillac!

K. Euthanasia of My Beloved Pet

During the summer of June, 2014-I brought Bentley, my beloved pet home with me. He resided in Chester, Va., with my daughter Pat- Pat. Bentley, and I became great friends, and we really relied on each other. Bentley would be so well-behaved when I would take him to get groomed- at the Pet Salon or for his comprehensive exam at the veterinary hospital. Many would tell me how great he was!

Then in 2019, Bentley's health began to decline. He began to get multiple skin irritations and he became partially blind. When I took him for his comprehensive exam in November 2021, it was noted that at this point- the only real option was to have him euthanized.

Of course this devastated me, but I did not want Bentley to suffer any longer. So, on December 2, 2021, my beloved Bentley was euthanized. I am so appreciative to my support system, who assisted me during this time. Mrs. Dee took me to dinner, Pat-Pat for the keepsake pillow, the veterinarian staff for a nice card and Bentley's paw prints, and Bec-Bec for the beautiful keepsake candle.

L. MEMORABLE KEEPSAKES

These memory keepsakes really helped me a lot after Bentley's passing. I look at them daily.

Bentley liked to dress up around Christmas time.

Every three months, I would take him to the groomers.

Bentley liked to spend time riding around in the car after getting groomed.

M. SALVATION/SENSE OF PEACE

Dear friends, I truly hoped that you enjoyed reading my book, as much as I enjoyed writing it. Even though, I endured many, many hardships and setbacks, I am glad to say that God has been there with me every step of the way. When I was terminated from my job, I continued to teach, acquiring 36 years in the profession-until my retirement on May 13, 2021. For the two car accidents that I have endured, to date-there has been no surgeries. When I was without a vehicle- God blessed me to be able to have 3 cars.

Even though I desired a Cadillac, God had something else in mind for me. A car that was easy on gas, low mileage, and little to no maintenance. God, has a way of placing the right people in your path at the right time. When Bentley was euthanized- of course I was upset the first week. But as the weeks went on, I began to feel a sense of calmness, in knowing that Bentley did not have to suffer any longer. The various keepsakes are great items to have as memorabilia.

Today, I can say that I have gained Salvation and a sense of peace. I am so thankful to God for sustaining me throughout all of my encounters. I am so reminded of my favorite scripture: PHLI. 4:13 "I CAN DO ALL THINGS THROUGH CHRIST WHICH STRENGTHENETH ME."

N. Annointed For Such A Time As This

I am thankful to God that His hands have been upon me since birth. I can clearly remember long ago- going to church with my mom and even being baptized at 10 years old! From those early years, the love of God was instilled in me, and it is still prevalent today. Of course we all have not always been on the straight and narrow and I will be the first to admit that, but look at the great work of God. I am proud to say that I am a mighty prayer warrior, intercessor, and an all-around generous person. I really get joy out of seeing others prosper, it gives me a good feeling!

O. Scriptures/Verses that Provided Peace

PEACE

"Now the Lord of peace himself give you peace always by all means. The Lord be with you all."
2 Thessalonians 3:16

"And the peace of God, which passeth all understanding, shall keep you hearts and minds through Christ Jesus." *Philippians 4:7*

"Peace I leave with you, my peace I give unto you: not as the world giveth, give I unto you. Let not your heart be troubled, neither let it be afraid." *John 14:27*

"In his days shall the righteous flourish; and abundance of peace so long as the moon endureth."
Psalm 72:7

"These *things* I have spoken unto you; that in me ye might have peace. In the world ye shall have tribulation: but be of good cheer; I have overcome the world." *John 16:33*

"I will both lay me down in peace, and sleep: for thou, LORD, only makest me dwell in safety."
Psalm 4:8

"And said, O man greatly beloved, fear not: peace *be* unto thee, be strong, yea, be strong. And when he had spoken unto me, I was strengthened, and said, Let my lord speak; for thou hast strengthened me." *Daniel 10:19*

P. QUESTIONS/NOTES ETC.

Were you released from work? If so, how did you manage and what scriptures helped you?

_____

_____

_____

_____

_____

_____

_____

_____

_____

_____

_____

_____

_____

_____

_____

_____

_____

_____

_____

_____

Have you ever been in a situation where you have had to euthanize a pet? What were some things that were helpful to you during this time?

_____

_____

_____

_____

_____

_____

_____

_____

_____

_____

_____

_____

_____

_____

_____

_____

_____

_____

_____

_____

Have you ever been in a car accident? If so, what was your experience like and how do you feel about your experience?

_____

_____

_____

_____

_____

_____

_____

_____

_____

_____

_____

_____

_____

_____

_____

_____

_____

_____

Share some life experiences that you have endured and God pull you out.

_____

_____

_____

_____

_____

_____

_____

_____

_____

_____

_____

_____

_____

_____

_____

_____

_____

_____

_____

_____

Did you enjoy reading my book? Express your thoughts here

_____

_____

_____

_____

_____

_____

_____

_____

_____

_____

_____

_____

_____

_____

_____

_____

_____

_____

_____

_____

I would like to take this time to thank my pastor, Bishop Bobby Weston, for the encouraging sermons that he would preach on Sundays and even in Bible Studies. They served as confirmation for me on many levels, and for that I am very appreciative. I also would like to thank Lady A for the great generosity and hospitality whenever I was in her presence. May God forever bless you all and your families!

Love always,
Miss Maxine

Printed in the United States
by Baker & Taylor Publisher Services